The REBU

Journaling
Preschool to Grade 1

Frank Schaffer Publications®

Send all inquiries to:
Frank Schaffer Publications
8720 Orion Place
Columbus, Ohio 43240-2111

Journaling the Rebus Way—Preschool to Grade 1

ISBN 0-7682-3469-7

2 3 4 5 6 7 8 9 10 PAT 12 11 10 09 08

Table of Contents

Published by Frank Schaffer Publications. Copyright protected.
0-7682-3469-7 *Journaling the Rebus Way*

How to Use This Book

Journaling the Rebus Way for Preschool to Grade 1 offers a unique approach to teaching children to read and write. Children will use the rebus method to learn new words and follow directions as they complete the activities on each page, thereby building on reading fundamentals while engaging directly with print.

Rebus describes a reading method where simple pictures appear along with, or in place of, the words they represent. In this book, we present the rebus pictures along with words in print to help children "read" print by giving them an extra support system. With this support system, children begin to recognize words that are part of their listening and speaking vocabulary but above their reading level.

Throughout this book, you will see that we use the same words and their rebus images repeatedly in the journal prompts. We carefully selected these twenty-four words for emergent readers and writers. Some of the words are common nouns that follow the *cvc* (consonant-vowel-consonant) pattern. This means that the words have short vowel sounds between two consonant letters. The words rhyme easily with other words in the same word family. For example, *cat* rhymes with *mat*, *hat*, and *rat*. Some of the words are nouns that provide important practice with common beginning and ending sounds, blends, and diphthongs, such as *house*, *night*, *rain*, and *school*. Repeated exposure to the words and their rebus images will help children to recognize the words in print.

The activities in this book also allow children to become familiar with commonly used direction words, such as *draw*, *circle*, *color*, and *trace*. These words are also illustrated as rebuses, allowing children to understand and complete the activities on their own. Drawing and writing activities allow for a deeper exposure to print and encourage children to express themselves.

The journal prompts in the book accommodate children of all learning abilities. Children who are just learning to write can draw a picture in response to a prompt. Then you can help them enter that picture and the corresponding word in the My Rebus Dictionary section of the book. More advanced learners can write complete sentences, relying on drawings only for words above their reading and writing level. Don't limit children to activities at their grade level. If a kindergartner finds the kindergarten prompts too easy, give him or her a prompt from the Grade 1 section. You can use the activities in this book in the order in which they appear or in any order that suits the needs of each child.

The Picture Dictionary in the back of this book features the twenty-four vocabulary words as well as the other concept words. The My Rebus Dictionary section allows children to create their own rebus-word pairs, using words from their own journal entries. Make copies of the Picture Dictionary and My Rebus Dictionary and laminate them for quick reference and review. You can use the reproducible flash cards in the back of the book for games, reference, drills, and review.

3

How to Use This Book, Continued

Throughout this book, you will see the following words and their corresponding rebuses:

ball   bed   bike   book   boy   brother

bus   cap   car   cat   day   dog

father   game   girl   house   mother   night

rain   school   sister   sun   toy   van

0-7682-3469-7 *Journaling the Rebus Way*

Using the Flash Cards

The flash cards for the twenty-four words featured in this book have the rebus image on one side and the corresponding word on the other. Provide note cards with other words, such as *the, a,* and *was.* Be sure to include simple adjectives as well. Children can use the note cards and the picture side of the flash cards to create their own rebus sentences, flipping over the flash cards to the word side as their skill level increases. You can also use the flash cards to play a variety of games. The games will help children recognize the words in a variety of contexts. You may wish to copy the flash cards onto heavy cardstock and laminate them.

Here are some suggestions for using the flash cards in a small group or one-on-one setting:

• Copy the picture side and word side of the cards onto separate pieces of paper. Cut out the flash cards. Lay down one picture card and two word cards (one with the picture name). Ask the child to find the word that names the picture.

• Select a Word of the Day from the flash cards. Talk about the word. Have the child use that word in a sentence. Post the word where the family or class can see it.

• Lay out three cards, word-side up. Be sure that two of the cards go together in some way (people words, place words, etc.). Ask the child to select the card that does not belong and explain why. Also have the child tell why the other two go together.

• Lay out six cards. Say a word, and ask the child to find a word that has the same beginning sound or ending sound as the word you said.

• Lay out several cards word-side up. Ask the child to select the card that answers a particular question. Ask: *Which one names a person?* or *Which one has wheels?*

• Use the flash cards as prompts for writing or storytelling. Put the cards in a basket and ask the child to pick one. Develop an idea around the word, and ask the child to write or draw something about the word.

• Pick out a flash card and ask the child to list words that rhyme with the word on the card. Make a list of the new words. Underline the letters that make the rhyme in each word. Circle the new letters at the beginning of each word.

Published by Frank Schaffer Publications. Copyright protected. 0-7682-3469-7 *Journaling the Rebus Way*

Preschool: All About Me

Write ✏️ your name.

_____

– – – – – – – – – – – – – – – – – – – –

My name is _____ .

Circle ✏️ the answer that describes you.

I am a   .
           boy   girl

I am **3   4   5   6** years old.

Published by Frank Schaffer Publications. Copyright protected.

0-7682-3469-7 *Journaling the Rebus Way*

Name _____ **Date** _____

Preschool: All About Me

Look in a mirror. Then, draw ✎ a picture of yourself.

Trace ✎ the word.

_____

— — — — — — — — — — — me — — —

_____

7

Preschool: All About Me

Color the van your favorite color.

Say  : The van is my favorite color.

Trace .... ✏ the word.

_____

- - - - - - - - - - - - van - - - - - - - - - - -

_____

8

Preschool: All About Me

Draw  a picture of something you like to do when the sun ☼ is out.

Say 👧 : This is what I like to do when the sun ☼ is out.

Trace ✏ the word.

sun

0-7682-3469-7 *Journaling the Rebus Way*

Preschool: All About Me

Where do you live? Draw a picture of your home.

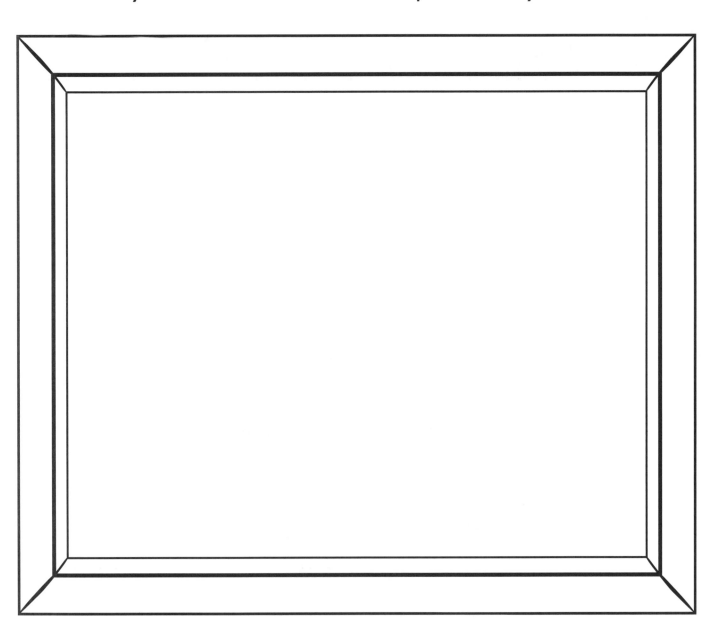

Say : This is my home.

0-7682-3469-7 *Journaling the Rebus Way*

Preschool: All About Me

Color the bed to look like your bed .

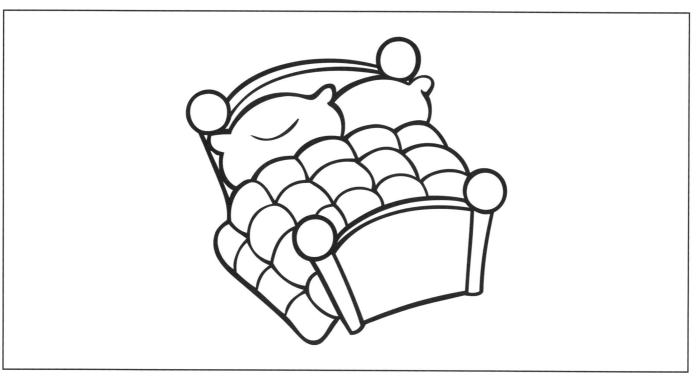

Say : This is my bed .

Trace ·····✎ the word.

b e d

0-7682-3469-7 *Journaling the Rebus Way*

Preschool: Family and Friends

Draw 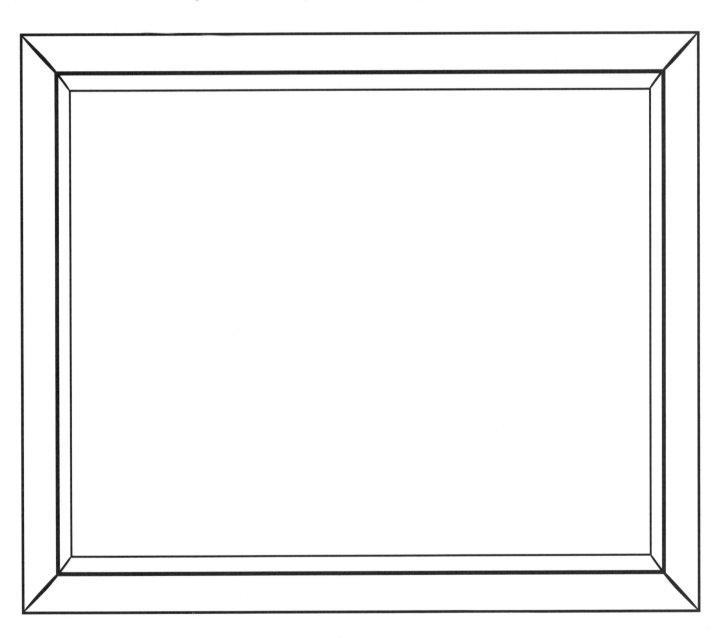 a picture of your family.

Say : This is my family.

0-7682-3469-7 *Journaling the Rebus Way*

Name _____   Date _____

Preschool: Family and Friends

Draw ✏️ a picture your family doing something fun together.

Say : This is my family having fun.

0-7682-3469-7 *Journaling the Rebus Way*

Preschool: Family and Friends

Draw ✏️ a picture of your family in the van 🚐 taking a trip.

Say 😊 : My family takes a trip.

Trace ✏️ the word.

_____

van

0-7682-3469-7 *Journaling the Rebus Way*

Preschool: Family and Friends

Draw  a picture of your friends.

Say : These are my friends.

0-7682-3469-7 *Journaling the Rebus Way*

Preschool: Family and Friends

Draw 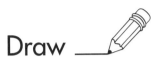 a picture of your friends playing with a toy .

Say : These are my friends playing with a toy .

Trace ✏ the word.

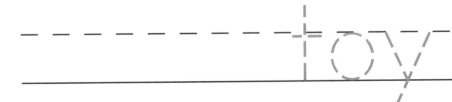

0-7682-3469-7 *Journaling the Rebus Way*

Preschool: Seasons

Draw  a picture of something you like to do in the winter.

0-7682-3469-7 *Journaling the Rebus Way*

Preschool: Seasons

Draw ✏️ a picture of something you like to do in the spring.

0-7682-3469-7 *Journaling the Rebus Way*

Preschool: Seasons

Draw ✏️ a picture of something you like to do in the summer.

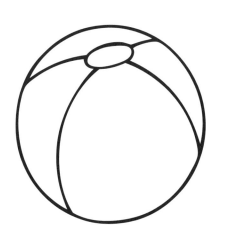

Published by **Frank Schaffer** Publications. Copyright protected.

Preschool: Seasons

Draw  a picture of something you like to do in the fall.

0-7682-3469-7 *Journaling the Rebus Way*

Preschool: Seasons

Draw 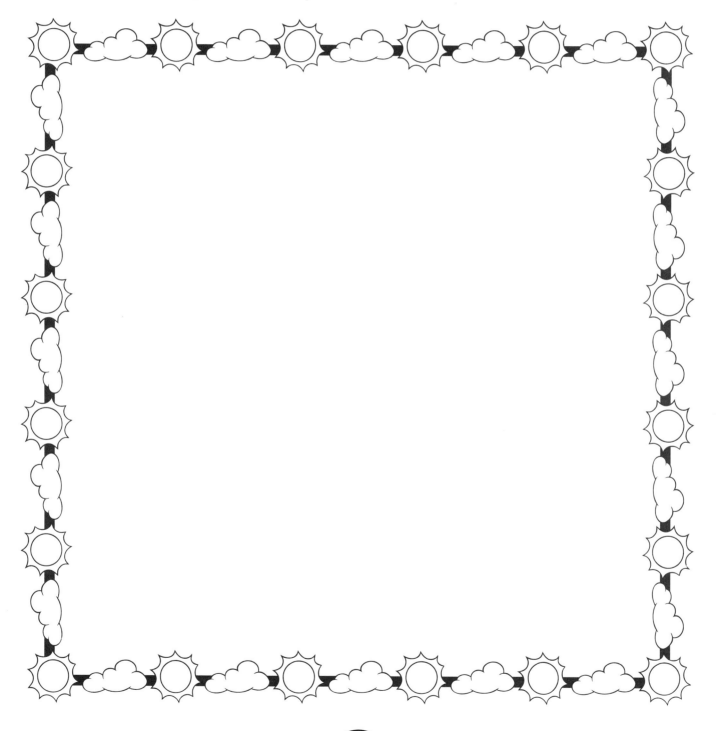 a picture of your favorite weather.

0-7682-3469-7 *Journaling the Rebus Way*

Preschool: Animals

Would you rather have a cat or a dog for a pet?

Color the pet you like better.

cat   **dog**

Say : I like this pet.

Trace ....🖉 the words.

0-7682-3469-7 *Journaling the Rebus Way*

Preschool: Animals

Draw ✏️ your pet or a pet you would like to have.

Trace ✏️ the word.

_____

- -

pet

_____

23

Preschool: Animals

Draw  a picture of your favorite zoo animal.

Write ✏ the zoo animal's name.

_____

– – – – – – – – – – – – – – – – – –

_____

Published by Frank Schaffer Publications. Copyright protected. 0-7682-3469-7 *Journaling the Rebus Way*

Preschool: Animals

Draw ✏ a picture of your favorite farm animal.

Write ✏ the farm animal's name.

_____

- -

_____

0-7682-3469-7 *Journaling the Rebus Way*

Preschool: Animals

Draw _____ a picture of the animal you would like to be.

Write _____ the name of the animal.

_____

- -

_____

0-7682-3469-7 *Journaling the Rebus Way*

Preschool: Just Pretend

Draw  a picture of yourself as a super hero.

Write your super hero name.

_____

- -

_____

0-7682-3469-7 *Journaling the Rebus Way*

Preschool: Just Pretend

Pretend you have 3 wishes. Draw ✏️ pictures to show what you would wish for.

0-7682-3469-7 *Journaling the Rebus Way*

Preschool: Just Pretend

Draw ✏️ a picture of what you would buy with a million dollars.

0-7682-3469-7 *Journaling the Rebus Way*

Preschool: Just Pretend

Pretend you have a magic cap . Draw a picture

to show what your magic cap can do?

Say : This is my cap .

Trace ⋯✏ the word.

_____

– – – – – – – – – – c a p – – – – –

0-7682-3469-7 *Journaling the Rebus Way*

Preschool: Just Pretend

Pretend one of your toys came to life. Draw a

picture of your toy .

Say : This is my toy .

31

Preschool: Community

Draw  a picture of the people who live close to you.

0-7682-3469-7 *Journaling the Rebus Way*

Preschool: Community

Draw  a picture of a police officer at work.

Trace ✏ the word.

_____

car

Published by Frank Schaffer Publications. Copyright protected.

0-7682-3469-7 *Journaling the Rebus Way*

Preschool: Community

Draw  a picture of a firefighter at work.

Published by Frank Schaffer Publications. Copyright protected.   0-7682-3469-7 *Journaling the Rebus Way*

Preschool: Community

Draw a picture of a mail carrier at work.

Color the letter.

Me
345 Short Street
Homesick, USA

My Friend
123 Long Street
Home Town, USA

0-7682-3469-7 *Journaling the Rebus Way*

Preschool: Community

Draw 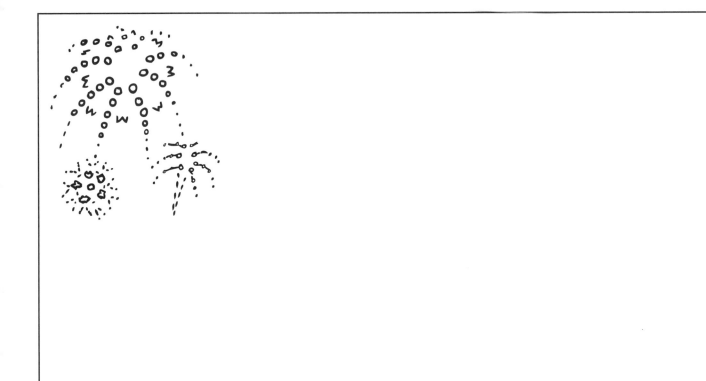 a picture of the July 4th celebration where you live.

Trace _____ the words.

0-7682-3469-7 *Journaling the Rebus Way*

Preschool: Community

Draw ✏️ a picture of a park.

0-7682-3469-7 *Journaling the Rebus Way*

Preschool: Community

Draw  a picture of a library.

Color the book .

0-7682-3469-7 *Journaling the Rebus Way*

Preschool: Community

Draw  a picture of a museum.

0-7682-3469-7 *Journaling the Rebus Way*

Preschool: Community

Draw  a picture of a hospital.

0-7682-3469-7 *Journaling the Rebus Way*

Preschool: Community

What can you do to help your community be a better place?

Draw  a picture of something you can do.

0-7682-3469-7 *Journaling the Rebus Way*

Kindergarten: All About Me

Write ✏ words to complete each sentence.

_____

_ _ _ _ _ _ _ _ _ _ _ _ _ _ _ _ _

My name is _____.

_____

_ _ _ _ _ _ _ _

I am _____ years old.

_____

_ _ _ _ _ _ _ _ _ _ _ _ _ _ _

My address is _____

_____

_ _ _ _ _ _ _ _ _ _ _ _ _ _ _ _ _

_____.

_____

_ _ _ _ _ _ _ _ _ _ _ _

My phone number is _____.

42

Kindergarten: All About Me

Look 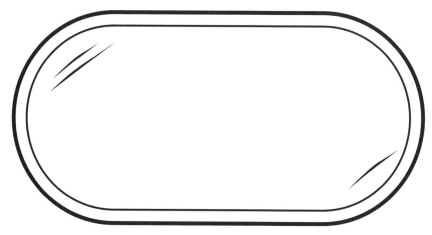 in a mirror. Write ✏️ words to complete each sentence.

_____

- -

I am a (girl 👧/boy 👦) _____.

_____

- -

My eyes are the color _____.

_____

- -

My hair is the color _____.

Draw ✏️ a picture
of your face.

43

0-7682-3469-7 *Journaling the Rebus Way*

Kindergarten: All About Me

What is your favorite color? Write  words to complete the sentence.

_____

– –

My favorite color is _____ .

Color ✏️ the bus 🚌 your favorite color.

0-7682-3469-7 *Journaling the Rebus Way*

Kindergarten: All About Me

What do you like to eat on a hot day when the sun is

out? Write _____ words to complete the sentence.

_____

- - - - - - - - - - - -

When it is hot, I like to eat _____

_____

- -

_____ .

Draw _____ a picture of yourself eating these foods.

0-7682-3469-7 *Journaling the Rebus Way*

Kindergarten: All About Me

Write your school's name to complete the sentence.

_____

- -

The name of my school is _____

_____

- -

_____.

Circle the answer to complete the sentence.

I _____ to school .

a) take the bus   **b)** go by car   **c)** walk

0-7682-3469-7 *Journaling the Rebus Way*

Kindergarten: All About Me

Write ✏️ a list of things that are in your room.

_____   _____

- - - - - - - - - - - - - - - - - -   - - - - - - - - - - - - - - - - - -

_____   _____

- - - - - - - - - - - - - - - - - -   - - - - - - - - - - - - - - - - - -

_____   _____

Draw ✏️ a picture of your bed .

0-7682-3469-7 *Journaling the Rebus Way*

Kindergarten: Family and Friends

Write _____ your family members' names below.

_____   _____

- - - - - - - - - - - - -   - - - - - - - - - - - - -

_____   _____

_____   _____

- - - - - - - - - - - - -   - - - - - - - - - - - - -

_____   _____

Draw _____ a picture of your family.

48

Kindergarten: Family and Friends

Pretend you are in charge of your family for a day.

Write ✏️ a sentence or a list of words describing the day.

_____

- -

_____

_____

- -

_____

Draw ✏️ a picture of your day in charge.

0-7682-3469-7 *Journaling the Rebus Way*

Name _____   Date _____

Kindergarten: Family and Friends

Think of a vacation you have taken with your family.

Write _____ the name of a place to complete the sentence.

_____

- -

My family went to _____

_____

- -

_____ .

Circle the answer to complete the sentence.

My family _____ on vacation.

a) went by bus   **b)** went by car   **c)** went by jet

     0-7682-3469-7 *Journaling the Rebus Way*

Kindergarten: Family and Friends

Who are your friends? Write _____ your friends' names below.

_____   _____

- - - - - - - - - - - - - -   - - - - - - - - - - - - - -

_____   _____

- - - - - - - - - - - - - -   - - - - - - - - - - - - - -

_____   _____

Draw _____ a picture of your friends.

0-7682-3469-7 *Journaling the Rebus Way*

Kindergarten: Family and Friends

What do your friends do for fun? Write ✏️ a sentence or a list of words about what your friends do for fun.

_____

- -

_____

_____

- -

_____

Draw ✏️ a picture of your friends doing something fun together.

Published by Frank Schaffer Publications. Copyright protected. 0-7682-3469-7 *Journaling the Rebus Way*

Name _____   **Date** _____

Kindergarten: Seasons

Write ✏️ words to complete each sentence.

_____

_ _ _ _ _ _ _ _ _ _ _ _ _ _ _

In the winter, it is _____ outside.

_____

_ _ _ _ _ _ _ _ _ _ _ _ _ _ _

In the winter, I like to _____.

_____

_ _ _ _ _ _ _ _ _ _ _ _ _ _ _

I like the winter because _____.

_____

_ _ _ _ _ _ _ _ _ _ _ _ _ _ _

I do not like the winter because _____

_____

_ _ _ _ _ _ _ _ _ _ _ _ _ _ _

_____.

Published by Frank Schaffer Publications. Copyright protected. 0-7682-3469-7 *Journaling the Rebus Way*

Kindergarten: Seasons

Write _____ a word or words complete each sentence.

_____

In the spring, it is _____ outside.

_____

In the spring, I like to _____.

_____

I like the spring because _____.

_____

I do not like the spring because _____

_____

_____

0-7682-3469-7 *Journaling the Rebus Way*

Kindergarten: Seasons

Write _____ a word or words to complete each sentence.

_____

_ _ _ _ _ _ _ _ _ _ _

In the summer, it is _____ outside.

_____

_ _ _ _ _ _ _ _ _ _ _ _

In the summer, I like to _____.

_____

_ _ _ _ _ _ _ _ _ _ _

I like the summer because _____.

_____

_ _ _ _ _ _ _ _ _

I do not like the summer because _____

_____

_ _ _ _ _ _ _ _ _ _ _ _ _ _ _ _ _

_____.

  0-7682-3469-7 *Journaling the Rebus Way*

Kindergarten: Seasons

Write ✏ a word or words to complete each sentence.

_____

– – – – – – – – – – –

In the fall, it is _____ outside.

_____

– – – – – – – – – – –

In the fall, I like to _____.

_____

– – – – – – – – – – –

I like the fall because _____.

_____

– – – – – – – – – – –

I do not like the fall because _____

_____

– – – – – – – – – – –

_____.

0-7682-3469-7 *Journaling the Rebus Way*

Kindergarten: Seasons

Write 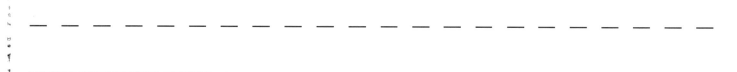 a sentence or a list of words about what you like to do when it rains.

_____

– –

_____

– –

_____

Draw _____ a picture of the rain.

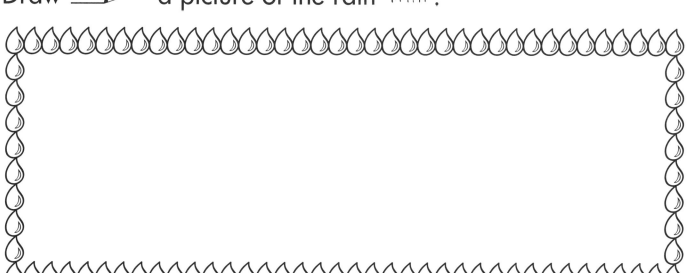

Published by Frank Schaffer Publications.   0-7682-3469-7 *Journaling the Rebus Way*

Kindergarten: Seasons

Write ✏️ a sentence or a list of words about what you like to do when it snows.

_____

_ _

_____

_ _

_____

Draw ✏️ a picture of the snow.

58

Kindergarten: Animals

Circle  the answer to complete the sentence.

The dog likes to play with a _____.

a) bus    **b)** car   **c)** ball

Write _____ a sentence about a dog that likes to play

with a ball .

_____

- - - - - - - - - - - - - - - - - - - -

_____

- - - - - - - - - - - - - - - - - - - -

_____

59

Kindergarten: Animals

Write ✎ a sentence or a list of words about your pet or a pet you would like to have.

_____

- - - - - - - - - - - - - - - - -

_____

- - - - - - - - - - - - - - - - -

_____

Draw ✏ a picture of the pet.

0-7682-3469-7 *Journaling the Rebus Way*

Kindergarten: Animals

Write ✏️ a sentence or a list of words about the zoo animal you like best.

_____

- -

_____

- -

_____

Draw ✏️ a picture of the zoo animal.

Published by Frank Schaffer Publications. Copyright protected.

0-7682-3469-7 *Journaling the Rebus Way*

Kindergarten: Animals

Write  a sentence or a list of words about the farm animal you like best.

_____

_ _

_____

_ _

_____

Draw _____ a picture of the farm animal.

0-7682-3469-7 *Journaling the Rebus Way*

Kindergarten: Animals

Write ✏ a word or words to complete the sentence.

_____

_ _ _ _ _ _ _ _ _ _ _ _ _

If I could be any animal, I would be a _____

_____

_ _

_____ .

_____

_ _ _ _ _ _ _ _ _ _ _ _ _

I would like to be this animal because _____

_____

_ _

_____

_____ .

63

Kindergarten: Just Pretend

Pretend you are a king or queen. Write ✏ a sentence or a list of words about being a king or queen.

_____

- - - - - - - - - - - - - - - - - - - -

_____

_____

- - - - - - - - - - - - - - - - - - - -

_____

Write ✏ words to complete the sentence.

If I were a king or queen, the name of my kingdom would be

_____

- - - - - - - - - - - - - - - - - - - -

_____

Published by Frank Schaffer Publications. Copyright protected. 0-7682-3469-7 *Journaling the Rebus Way*

Kindergarten: Just Pretend

Pretend you have to cook a meal. Write words to complete each sentence.

_____

- - - - - - - - - - - -

If I had to cook a meal, I would cook _____.

To cook this meal, I have to

_____

- - - - - - - - - - - - - - - - -

1. _____

_____

- - - - - - - - - - - - - - - -

2. _____

_____

- - - - - - - - - - - - - - - -

3. _____

0-7682-3469-7 *Journaling the Rebus Way*

Kindergarten: Just Pretend

Pretend you have a million dollars. Write  a list of the things you would buy.

_____   _____

- - - - - - - - - -   - - - - - - - - - -

_____   _____

_____   _____

- - - - - - - - - -   - - - - - - - - - -

_____   _____

Draw _____ a picture of your things.

     0-7682-3469-7 *Journaling the Rebus Way*

Kindergarten: Just Pretend

Pretend you have a magic car  that can fly. Where would

you fly to? Write a sentence or a list of words about

your flying car .

_____

\- \- \- \- \- \- \- \- \- \- \- \- \- \- \- \-

_____

\- \- \- \- \- \- \- \- \- \- \- \- \- \- \- \-

_____

Color the car to look like your flying car .

0-7682-3469-7 *Journaling the Rebus Way*

Kindergarten: Just Pretend

Pretend you live on the sun . What would it be like?

Write _____ words to complete each sentence.

_____

- - - - - - - -

I would like to live on the sun because _____

_____

- -

_____ .

_____

- - - - - - - -

I would not like to live on the sun because _____

_____

- -

_____ .

0-7682-3469-7 *Journaling the Rebus Way*

Kindergarten: Community

Who are your neighbors? Write _____ a sentence or a list of words about the people who live close to you.

_____

\- \- \- \- \- \- \- \- \- \- \- \- \- \- \- \- \- \- \- \-

_____

\- \- \- \- \- \- \- \- \- \- \- \- \- \- \- \- \- \- \- \-

_____

Draw _____ a picture of your street and the house or home where your neighbors live.

0-7682-3469-7 *Journaling the Rebus Way*

Kindergarten: Community

What does a police officer do? Write _____ words to complete each sentence.

_____

- - - - - -

A police officer has an important job because _____

_____

- -

_____ .

_____

- - - - - -

To do his or her job, a police officer needs _____

_____

- -

_____ .

_____

- - - - - -

A police officer wears _____ .

70

Kindergarten: Community

What does a firefighter do? Write ✏ words to complete each sentence.

_____

- - - - - - - - - - - - - - -

A firefighter has an important job because _____

_____

- - - - - - - - - - - - - - -

_____ .

_____

- - - - - - - - - - - - - - -

To do his or her job, a firefighter needs _____

_____

- - - - - - - - - - - - - - -

_____ .

_____

- - - - - - - - - - - - - - -

A firefighter wears _____ .

71

Kindergarten: Community

What does a mail carrier do? Write words to complete each sentence.

_____

_ _ _ _ _ _

A mail carrier has an important job because _____

_____

_ _ _ _ _ _ _ _ _ _ _ _

_____.

_____

_ _ _ _ _ _ _

To do his or her job, a mail carrier needs _____

_____

_ _ _ _ _ _ _ _ _ _ _ _

_____.

_____

_ _ _ _ _ _ _

A mail carrier wears _____.

72

0-7682-3469-7 *Journaling the Rebus Way*

Kindergarten: Community

Write ✏️ a sentence or a list of words about the July 4th celebration where you live.

_____

- -

_____

_____

- -

_____

Draw ✏️ a picture of July 4th fireworks.

0-7682-3469-7 *Journaling the Rebus Way*

Kindergarten: Community

Is there a park where you live? Write _____ words to complete each sentence.

_____

– –

At the park, I see _____ .

_____

– –

At the park, I hear _____ .

_____

– –

At the park, I like to _____ .

_____

– –

At the park, I do not like to _____ .

0-7682-3469-7 *Journaling the Rebus Way*

Kindergarten: Community

What do you do at the library? Write ✏️ a sentence or a list of words about the library.

_____

- -

_____

- -

_____

Draw  a picture of the librarian at the library.

     0-7682-3469-7 *Journaling the Rebus Way*

Kindergarten: Community

What do you do at the museum? Write  a sentence or a list of words about the museum.

_____

- -

_____

_____

- -

_____

Draw _____ a picture that could go into a museum.

0-7682-3469-7 *Journaling the Rebus Way*

Kindergarten: Community

What happens at a hospital? Write ✎ a sentence or a list of words about a hospital.

_____

- -

_____

- -

_____

Draw ✏ a picture of a doctor or a nurse at a hospital.

0-7682-3469-7 *Journaling the Rebus Way*

Kindergarten: Community

What can you do to help your community be a better place?

Write ✏ words to complete each sentence.

Planting a tree would help my community because
_____

- -

_____

_____

- -

_____ .

Picking up litter would help my community because
_____

- -

_____

_____

- -

_____ .

0-7682-3469-7 *Journaling the Rebus Way*

Grade 1: All About Me

Write _____ complete sentences to answer each question.

_____

- - - - - - - - - - - - - - - - - -

What is your full name? _____

_____

- - - - - - - - - - - - - - - - - -

_____

_____

- - - - - - - - - - - - - - - - - -

_____

_____

- - - - - - - - - - - - - - - - - -

How old are you? _____

_____

- - - - - - - - - - - - - - - - - -

_____

0-7682-3469-7 *Journaling the Rebus Way*

Grade 1: All About Me

Write complete sentences to answer each question.

_____

Are you a boy or a girl ? _____

_____

- - - - - - - - - - - - - - -

_____

_____

- - - - - - - - - - - - - - -

What do you look like? _____

_____

- - - - - - - - - - - - - - -

_____

_____

- - - - - - - - - - - - - - -

_____

0-7682-3469-7 *Journaling the Rebus Way*

Grade 1: All About Me

What does your house or home look like? Write

a sentence about your house or home.

_____

- -

_____

_____

- -

_____

Draw a picture of your house or home.

0-7682-3469-7 *Journaling the Rebus Way*

Grade 1: All About Me

Write complete sentences to answer each question.

What is your favorite game to play? _____

- -

_____

_____

- -

_____

Why is this your favorite game ? _____

- -

_____

_____

- -

_____

Published by Frank Schaffer Publications. Copyright protected.   0-7682-3469-7 *Journaling the Rebus Way*

Grade 1: All About Me

Write complete sentences to answer each question.

What school 🏫 do you go to?

_____

- -

_____

_____

- -

_____

What is your teacher's name?

_____

- -

_____

_____

- -

_____

83

Name _____   Date _____

Grade 1: All About Me

Write complete sentences to answer each question.

What is your favorite book ?

_____

- -

_____

_____

- -

_____

Why is it your favorite book ?

_____

- -

_____

_____

- -

_____

Published by Frank Schaffer Publications. Copyright protected.   0-7682-3469-7 *Journaling the Rebus Way*

Grade 1: Family and Friends

Write complete sentences to answer each question.

What is your mother's name?

_____

- -

_____

_____

- -

_____

What is your father's name?

_____

- -

_____

_____

- -

_____

Published by Frank Schaffer Publications. Copyright protected.
0-7682-3469-7 *Journaling the Rebus Way*

Grade 1: Family and Friends

Write complete sentences to answer each question.

Do you have a brother ? If so, what is his name?

_ _

_____

_ _

_____

Do you have a sister ? If so, what is her name?

_ _

_____

_ _

86

Grade 1: Family and Friends

Write ✏️ two or three sentences about a holiday party you have shared with your family. Use the words

mother 👨‍👩‍👧‍👦, **father** 👨‍👩‍👧‍👦, **day** ☀️, and

night 🌙 .

_____

_ _ _ _ _ _ _ _ _ _ _ _ _ _ _ _ _ _ _

_____

_ _ _ _ _ _ _ _ _ _ _ _ _ _ _ _ _ _ _

_____

_ _ _ _ _ _ _ _ _ _ _ _ _ _ _ _ _ _ _

_____

_ _ _ _ _ _ _ _ _ _ _ _ _ _ _ _ _ _ _

_____

87

Grade 1: Family and Friends

Write _____ complete sentences to answer each question.

What is the name of one of your friends?

_____

_ _

_____

_ _

_____

What do you like about your friend?

_____

_ _

_____

_ _

_____

88

Grade 1: Family and Friends

Write two or three sentences about your last birthday party. Did you invite your friends? Did you invite your family?

Use the words **boy** or **girl** , **toy** , and

game .

_____

_ _

_____

_ _

_____

_ _

_____

_ _

_____

    0-7682-3469-7 *Journaling the Rebus Way*

Grade 1: Seasons

Write ✏ complete sentences to answer each question.

What do you like about the winter?

_____

- -

_____

- -

_____

What do you not like about the winter?

_____

- -

_____

- -

_____

Published by Frank Schaffer Publications. Copyright protected.
0-7682-3469-7 *Journaling the Rebus Way*

Grade 1: Seasons

Write _____ complete sentences to answer each question.

What do you like about the spring?

_____

- -

_____

- -

_____

What do you not like about the spring?

_____

- -

_____

- -

_____

0-7682-3469-7 *Journaling the Rebus Way*

Grade 1: Seasons

Write ✏️ complete sentences to answer each question.

What do you like about the summer?

_____

_____

_____

_____

What do you not like about the summer?

_____

_____

_____

_____

0-7682-3469-7 *Journaling the Rebus Way*

Grade 1: Seasons

Write _____ complete sentences to answer each question.

What do you like about the fall?

_____

_____

_____

_____

What do you not like about the fall?

_____

_____

_____

_____

0-7682-3469-7 *Journaling the Rebus Way*

Grade 1: Seasons

Write _____ complete sentences to answer each question.

_____

- -

What is night like? _____

_____

- -

_____

_____

- -

What happens at night ? _____

_____

- -

_____

_____

- -

_____

0-7682-3469-7 *Journaling the Rebus Way*

Grade 1: Seasons

Write complete sentences to answer each question.

_____

- - - - - - - - - - - - - - - - - - -

What is day like? _____

_____

- - - - - - - - - - - - - - - - - - -

_____

_____

- - - - - - - - - - - - - - - - - - -

What happens during the day ? _____

_____

- - - - - - - - - - - - - - - - - - -

_____

_____

- - - - - - - - - - - - - - - - - - -

_____

   0-7682-3469-7 *Journaling the Rebus Way*

Grade 1: Animals

Write _____ two or three sentences about your favorite animal. Why is it your favorite animal?

_____

- -

_____

_____

- -

_____

_____

- -

_____

- -

_____

0-7682-3469-7 *Journaling the Rebus Way*

Grade 1: Animals

Write [pencil] two or three sentences about your least favorite animal. Why is it your least favorite animal?

0-7682-3469-7 *Journaling the Rebus Way*

Grade 1: Animals

Write ✏ complete sentences to answer each question.

Have you ever been to a zoo? If so, what was the zoo like? If not, what do you think a zoo would be like?

_____

- -

_____

- -

_____

Would you like to be a zookeeper? Why or why not?

_____

- -

_____

- -

_____

98

Grade 1: Animals

Write ✏ complete sentences to answer each question.

Have you ever been to a farm? If so, what was the farm like? If not, what do you think a farm would be like?

_____

- -

_____

- -

_____

Would you like to be a farmer? Why or why not?

_____

- -

_____

- -

_____

0-7682-3469-7 *Journaling the Rebus Way*

Grade 1: Animals

Write complete sentences to answer each question.

Would you rather be a cat or a dog ?

_ _

_____

_ _

_____

What is similar about a dog and a cat ?

_ _

_____

_ _

_____

Published by Frank Schaffer Publications. Copyright protected.   0-7682-3469-7 Journaling the Rebus Way

Grade 1: Just Pretend

Pretend you are a grownup. What are you like? What is your job? Write two or three sentences about yourself as a grownup. Use the words **mother** or **father** and **car** 🚗.

_____

_____

_____

_____

_____

_____

_____

_____

_____

_____

0-7682-3469-7 _Journaling the Rebus Way_

Grade 1: Just Pretend

Pretend you are a famous athlete. What sport do you play?

How did you become so good at this sport? Write two or three sentences about yourself as a famous athlete. Use the

words **ball** , **cap** , and **game** .

_____

- -

_____

- -

_____

- -

_____

- -

_____

102

Grade 1: Just Pretend

Pretend you have a magic bike 🚲. What does this magic

bike 🚲 do? Write two or three sentences about your magic

bike 🚲.

_____

- -

_____

- -

_____

- -

_____

- -

_____

0-7682-3469-7 *Journaling the Rebus Way*

Grade 1: Just Pretend

Pretend you are the President of the United States.

Write ✏ complete sentences to answer each question.

What would you like to do as the president?

_ _

_____

_ _

_____

Who would you like to meet as the president?

_ _

_____

_ _

_____

Published by Frank Schaffer Publications. Copyright protected.   0-7682-3469-7 *Journaling the Rebus Way*

Grade 1: Just Pretend

Pretend you are the teacher of your class for a day.

Write two or three sentences about your day. Use the

words **school** , **game** , and **book** .

_____

- -

_____

_____

- -

_____

_____

- -

_____

0-7682-3469-7 *Journaling the Rebus Way*

Grade 1: Community

Who are your neighbors? Write two or three sentences about your favorite neighbor. What do you like about this neighbor? Use the words **girl** or **boy**

and **house** .

_____

_ _

_____

_ _

_____

_ _

_____

Published by Frank Schaffer Publications. Copyright protected.   0-7682-3469-7 *Journaling the Rebus Way*

Grade 1: Community

What does a police officer do? Write ✏ complete sentences to answer each question.

Why does your community need police officers?

_ _

_____

_____

_ _

_____

What have you seen a police officer doing in your community?

_ _

_____

_____

_ _

_____

0-7682-3469-7 *Journaling the Rebus Way*

Grade 1: Community

What does a firefighter do? Write ✏️ complete sentences to answer each question.

Why does your community need firefighters?

_____

- -

_____

- -

_____

What have you seen a firefighter doing in your community?

_____

- -

_____

- -

_____

0-7682-3469-7 *Journaling the Rebus Way*

Grade 1: Community

What does a mail carrier do? Write ✏ complete sentences to answer each question.

Why does your community need a mail carrier?

_____

- -

_____

- -

_____

What have you seen a mail carrier doing in your community?

- -

_____

_____

- -

_____

0-7682-3469-7 *Journaling the Rebus Way*

Grade 1: Community

What does your community do for July 4th? Write two
or three sentences about the July 4th celebration where you

live. Use the words **car** , **night** , and **sun** .

_____

- -

_____

- -

_____

- -

_____

- -

_____

- -

_____

0-7682-3469-7 *Journaling the Rebus Way*

Grade 1: Community

Is there a park where you live? Write a story about a park. Use the words **ball** , **bike** , and **day** .

_____

- -

_____

- -

_____

_____

- -

_____

_____

- -

_____

0-7682-3469-7 *Journaling the Rebus Way*

Grade 1: Community

Is there a library where you live? Answer each question with complete sentences.

What things do you find in the library? _____

_____

_____

_____

What different things can you do at the library? _____

_____

_____

_____

112

 0-7682-3469-7 *Journaling the Rebus Way*

Grade 1: Community

Is there a museum where you live? Answer each question with complete sentences.

What things do you find in a museum?

_____

- -

_____

_____

- -

_____

What different things can you do at a museum?

_____

- -

_____

_____

- -

_____

0-7682-3469-7 *Journaling the Rebus Way*

Grade 1: Community

Is there a hospital where you live? Answer each question with complete sentences.

What happens in a hospital?

_____

_ _

_____

_____

_ _

_____

Who works at a hospital?

_____

_ _

_____

_____

_ _

_____

Published by Frank Schaffer Publications. Copyright protected.   0-7682-3469-7 *Journaling the Rebus Way*

Grade 1: Community

What can you do to help your community be a better place?

Write two or three sentences about things you can do

to help your community. Use the words **bus** ,

bike , and **school** .

_____

- -

_____

- -

_____

- -

_____

- -

_____

0-7682-3469-7 *Journaling the Rebus Way*

More Writing Prompts

Additional writing prompts include:

My favorite clothes are...
My favorite book is...
My home town is...
Sometimes I feel...
I wish I could...
I do not like to...
I think it is funny when...
I wonder about...
I worry about...
I am thankful for...
I feel lucky when...
My favorite sport is...
My favorite time of day is...
The best thing about...
I would like to see...
I know a lot about...
I want to learn about...
I am happy when...
I love the smell of...
I love the feel of...

I love the sound of...
I love the taste of...
The best thing that ever happened to me is...
The worst thing that ever happened to me is...
I am proud of...
If I made the rules at my house...
If I was a crayon...
If I was a flower...
If I lived in a tree house...
Three reasons why I should not eat my vegetables are...
Three reasons why I should not to take my bath are...
My grandmother...
My grandfather...
I like myself because...

Published by Frank Schaffer Publications. Copyright protected.

0-7682-3469-7 *Journaling the Rebus Way*

Picture Dictionary

This picture dictionary will help young learners become familiar with the rebuses used in this book. It is organized in the same order in which the words are introduced in the book. Use this picture dictionary for reference and review.

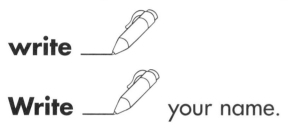

write

Write your name.

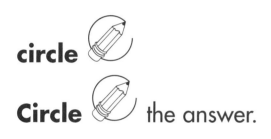

circle

Circle the answer.

boy

That **boy** is in my class.

girl

My sister is a little

girl .

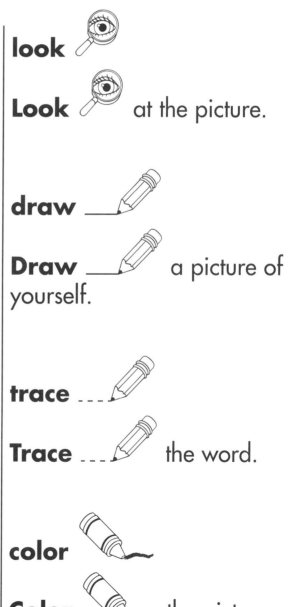

look

Look at the picture.

draw

Draw a picture of yourself.

trace

Trace the word.

color

Color the picture.

0-7682-3469-7 *Journaling the Rebus Way*

Picture Dictionary

van
We rode to the store in our

van .

say

Say : I like to eat.

sun

The **sun** makes me feel warm and happy!

bed

My **bed**  is soft.

toy
I think my robot is my favorite

toy .

cat

I think a **cat** is a good pet.

dog

My **dog** just buried a bone in the yard.

cap
I cannot find my baseball

cap .

118

0-7682-3469-7 *Journaling the Rebus Way*

Picture Dictionary

car

My mother had to put

gas in her **car** .

book

That **book** has some funny animal stories.

bus

The **bus** takes me home.

school
I'm learning to count at

school .

rain

The **rain** was pouring down on the sidewalk.

ball
I hit a home run with the

ball .

house

My friend's **house** is next to mine.

game

I like to play a **game** like checkers.

0-7682-3469-7 *Journaling the Rebus Way*

Picture Dictionary

mother

My **mother** bakes the best chocolate cake!

father

I helped my **father** cut the grass.

brother

My **brother** plays sports after school.

sister

My **sister** plays the piano.

day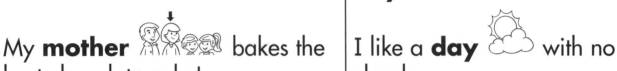

I like a **day** with no clouds.

night

I see the moon when the sky gets dark at **night** .

bike

My new **bike** is blue and white.

0-7682-3469-7 *Journaling the Rebus Way*

My Rebus Dictionary

Make your own Rebus Dictionary. Draw _____ pictures of

important words from your journal entries. Write _____ the
word to go with each picture.

 0-7682-3469-7 *Journaling the Rebus Way*

My Rebus Dictionary

0-7682-3469-7 *Journaling the Rebus Way*

ball	**bed**
bike	**book**
boy	**brother**
bus	**cap**

0-7682-3469-7 *Journaling the Rebus Way*

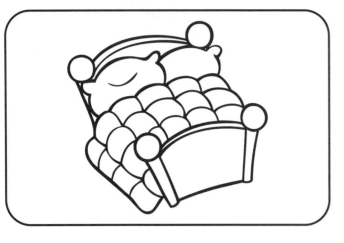

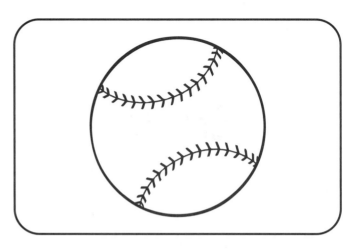

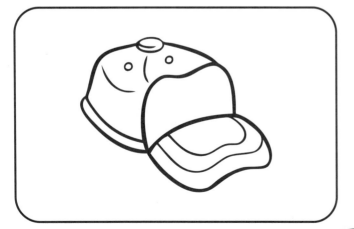

SCHOOL BUS

0-7682-3469-7 *Journaling the Rebus Way*

car

cat

day

dog

father

game

girl

house

Published by Frank Schaffer Publications. 0-7682-3469-7 *Journaling the Rebus Way*

0-7682-3469-7 *Journaling the Rebus Way*

mother	night
rain	school
sister	sun
toy	van

0-7682-3469-7 *Journaling the Rebus Way*

0-7682-3469-7 *Journaling the Rebus Way*

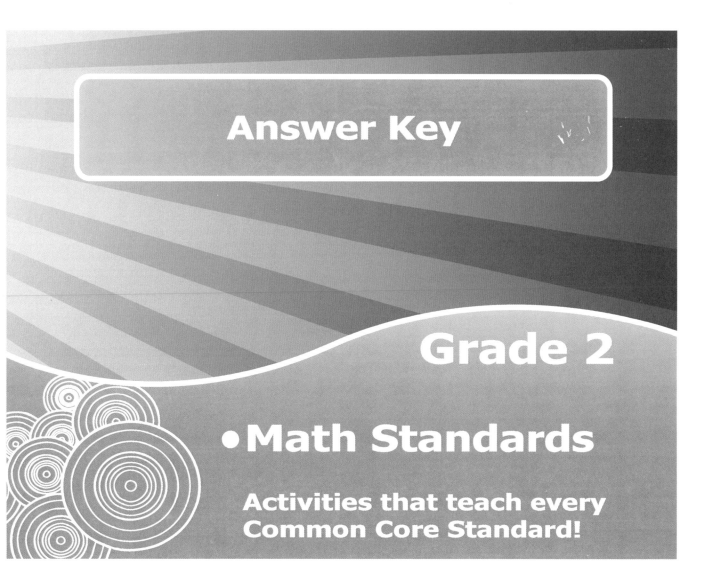

Common Core
State Standards

Answer Key

Grade 2

•Math Standards

**Activities that teach every
Common Core Standard!**

2

CoreCommonStandards.com

MATH STANDARDS
Pages 5-330

2.OA.1 : Pages 5-16

BARNYARD MATH
Practice answering the word problems. Students can play the Tic-Tac-Toe game, draw it, or both. After, practice these skills on the worksheet. Draw pictures to support the equations.
From top to bottom...
3+2+5=10 (Letter O)
7+2+4=13 (Letter D)
2+10+4=16 (Letter Y)
20+14=34 (Letter M)
Therefore, using those letters and numbers, the answer to the joke is M-O-O-D-Y. The grouchy cow is Moo-dy.

2.OA.2 : Pages 17-26

LET'S WORKOUT OUR BRAIN
Use the card game to practice adding and subtracting.

2.OA.3 : Pages 27-42

ODD OR EVEN
Count the items on the picture cards to sort them into odds and evens.

ODDS OR EVENS (APPLES)
ODDS: 3, 7, 13, 11, 15, 1, 19 (color brown)
EVENS: 14, 8, 2, 4, 10, 6, 18 (color red)

2.OA.4 : Pages 43-56

SWEET RECTANGULAR ARRAYS
Match the cupcake cards to the equation cards that fit. Practice that skill on the worksheet.
Answers from top to bottom...

PICTURE COLUMN:	EQUATION:
2 rows of 4	4+4=8
2 rows of 5	5+5=10
5 rows of 2	2+2+2+2+2=10
2 rows of 2	2+2=4
3 rows of 3	3+3+3=9
4 rows of 3	3+3+3+3=12

2.NBT.1 : Pages 57-68

LET'S MAKE A NUMBER!
Play the game to practice place value. Directions are on page 57.

2.NBT.2 : Pages 69-74

SKIP COUNTING WITH APPLES
Cut the 9 puzzle pieces out. The answers are on the adjacent piece. Fill in the blanks and check your answers.

WHAT COMES NEXT?
ROW 1: 35, 40
ROW 2: 20, 22
ROW 3: 110, 120
ROW 4: 18, 19
Answers will vary for the last 2 rows.

2.NBT.3 : Pages 75-92

BLAST OFF WITH NUMBERS
Match the expanded form, the written form, and the number form cards together. Practice that skill on the worksheet on page 392.

EXPANDED:	BASE 10:	WORD FORM:
300+50+0	350	Three Hundred Fifty
700+40+3	743	Seven Hundred Forty-Three
200+80+2	282	Two Hundred Eighty-Two
100+30+9	139	One Hundred Thirty-Nine
700+20	720	Seven Hundred Twenty
800+70+5	875	Eight Hundred Seventy-Five
600+90+3	693	Six Hundred Ninety-Three

2.NBT.4 : Pages 93-112

SUPER HERO COMPARING NUMBERS
Use the cards to play WAR the card game. Use page 405 to record battles and number comparisons.

2.NBT.5 : Pages 113-126

LET'S GO ON A TRIP!
Use the spinner and cards to play a game. Add or subtract the two numbers to compare. Keep track on the record sheet on page 117. Practice more on page 125.
Answers from left to right...

COLUMN 1:	COLUMN 2:	COLUMN 3:
98	100	74
44	67	*Answers vary.*

2.NBT.6 : Pages 127-150

ADDING TWO-DIGIT NUMBERS
Practice adding with the number cards. Add 2 or more numbers together, using the worksheet for practice.

2.NBT.7 : Pages 151-168

ADD AND SUBTRACT WITH FROGS
Use the cards to practice adding and subtracting 3-digit numbers. Write down problems and answers on page 446. The first few framed pages are large examples that can be use to practice as a group.

2.NBT.8 : Pages 169-184

POPCORN MENTAL MATH
Use the red popcorn cards and the blue popcorn cards to practice adding and subtracting 3-digit numbers. Write down problems and answers on the worksheet.

2.NBT.9 : Pages 185-190
WHY DOES IT WORK?
Use these pages to practice explaining why answers work.

2.MD.1 : Pages 191-202
MEASURE IT!
Use the question cards and appropriate measuring tools to measure the items on the cards. Write answers on page 193.

2.MD.2 : Pages 203-208
CENTIMETERS AND INCHES
Use two measures to find the length of the items on the cards.

2.MD.3 : Pages 209-216
ESTIMATE AND MEASURE
Put estimates of lengths for each unit. Some units might not be applicable to the item, and could be marked with an X or left blank.

2.MD.4 : Pages 217-224
MEASURE IT!
Use the cards to choose two objects. Measure them and compare the differences in lengths. Record your answers on the worksheet to compare.

2.MD.5 : Pages 225-240
ICE FISHING WITH SAM AND JAKE
Practice illustrating to solve problems. Sample answers:
229: 5 inches + 6 inches longer = 11 inch fish
231: 17 feet + 19 feet = 36 feet
233: 29 feet - 22 feet = 7 feet
235: 15 inches + 5 inches = 20 inches
237: 31 inches - 19 inches = 12 inches
239: 50 minutes + 30 minutes = 80 minutes

2.MD.6 : Pages 241-262
LET'S USE A NUMBER LINE
Assemble a number line. Start at 50. Shuffle through cards, take turns drawing and moving to jump forward or back. Keep track on your record sheet.

2.MD.7 : Pages 263-278
WHAT TIME IS IT?
Use the clocks and their hands, as well as the time cards to practice showing different times on the clocks.

WHAT TIME IS IT
Draw the hands on the clocks to indicate the proper times.

2.MD.8 : Pages 279-288
LET'S GO SHOPPING
Use the money manipulatives to help answer questions on page 539. Answers from left to right...

COL1:	COL2:	COL3:	COL4:	COL5:
40 cents	51 cents	25 cents	65 cents	$1.05
#3.50	$1.00	$1.20	$1.02	32 cents

2.MD.9 : Pages 289-298
MEASURE AND PLOT
Using the cards, do some measurements. For each one, place an X on the plot. Do several to generate some variety.

2.MD.10 : Pages 299-304
LET'S MAKE A BAR GRAPH
Use information from your classmates to make a pictograph and a bar graph. Answer the questions on the bar graph page also.

2.G.1 : Pages 305-312
MAGIC SHAPES
Use the shapes cards to ask each other questions. Move steps on the board according to how many points are left after each clue is given.

2.G.2 : Pages 313-318
SHARING CHOCOLATE
Practice cutting page 569 into different sizes, according to the number rolled on dice. Then practice drawing cuts on the chocolate bars on the worksheet. The number in the box tells you how many pieces to cut it into.
Answers are given in possible cutting styles, as each piece must be the same size. They are arrays, really. Answers from left to right:

COLUMN 1:	COLUMN 2:	COLUMN 3:
6=1x6, 3x2, 2x3	5=1x5	3=1x3
10=1x10, 2x5, 5x2	7=1x7	9=1x9, 3x3
2=1x2	4=1x4, 2x2	8=1x8, 2x4, 4x2

2.G.3 : Pages 319-330
PIZZA FOR ALL!
Practice using fraction pieces and adding fractions with the activities on these pages.

Common Core State Standards
Educating classrooms one standard at a time.

Terms of Use

All worksheets, activities, workbooks and other printable materials purchased or downloaded from this website are protected under copyright law. Items purchased from this website may be used, copied and printed for classroom, personal and home use depending on how many licenses are purchased. Upon printing and copying the materials from this website, you must leave the Copyright Information at the bottom of each item printed. Items may not be copied or distributed unless you have purchased them from this website. Furthermore, you may not reproduce, sell, or copy these resources, or post on your website any Worksheet, Activity, PDF, Workbook, or Printable without written permission from Have Fun Teaching, LLC using the contact form below. All Common Core State Standards are from CoreStandards.org and the Common Core State Standards Initiative.

All Common Core State Standards in this book are © Copyright 2010. National Governors Association Center for Best Practices and Council of Chief State School Officers. All rights reserved. Furthermore, NGA Center/CCSSO are the sole owners and developers of the Common Core State Standards, and Core Common Standards makes no claims to the contrary.

All Graphics, Images, and Logos are © Copyright 2012 CoreCommonStandards.com. Also, the organization of this book and Table of Contents has been created by and organized by CoreCommonStandards.com and HaveFunTeaching.com.

Fore more Common Core Standards Posters, Activities, Worksheets, and Workbooks, visit http://CoreCommonStandards.com.

Worksheets created by: Have Fun Teaching
Activities created by: Have Fun Teaching
Posters created by: Have Fun Teaching

334

Made in the USA
Monee, IL
11 April 2020